Other works published by the author, available from iUniverse:

A Bell Curve and Other Poems (2013)
An Artist's Model and Other Poems (2012)
Black Hole and Other Poems (2012)
Pursuit and Other Poems (2011)
Persistence and Other Poems (2010)
Celebrations and Other Poems (2009)
War-Wise and Other Poems (2009)
Surface Tension and Other Poems (2008)
Confusion Matrix and Other Poems (2007)

An Apology
AND *Other Poems*

DAVID J. MURRAY

iUniverse

AN APOLOGY AND OTHER POEMS

Copyright © 2016 David Murray.

All rights reserved. No part of this book may be used or reproduced by any means, graphic, electronic, or mechanical, including photocopying, recording, taping or by any information storage retrieval system without the written permission of the author except in the case of brief quotations embodied in critical articles and reviews.

iUniverse books may be ordered through booksellers or by contacting:

iUniverse
1663 Liberty Drive
Bloomington, IN 47403
www.iuniverse.com
1-800-Authors (1-800-288-4677)

Because of the dynamic nature of the Internet, any web addresses or links contained in this book may have changed since publication and may no longer be valid. The views expressed in this work are solely those of the author and do not necessarily reflect the views of the publisher, and the publisher hereby disclaims any responsibility for them.

Any people depicted in stock imagery provided by Thinkstock are models, and such images are being used for illustrative purposes only.
Certain stock imagery © Thinkstock.

ISBN: 978-1-4917-8647-5 (sc)
ISBN: 978-1-4917-8648-2 (hc)
ISBN: 978-1-4917-8646-8 (e)

Print information available on the last page.

iUniverse rev. date: 1/26/2016

Contents

Introduction ix
Preamble: All I Can Do xi

Apologies

An Apology 3
Apology #2 4
Apology #3 5
Apology #4 6
Remorse 7

Sprawl - Verses

Glitter and Gloss 11
Relativity Theory 12
Meeting 13
To the Sun 14

Dangers

Eye Contact 17
My Blast of Colour and Delight 18
The Psychopathology of Everyday Life 19
Female Eyes 20
My Model 21
First Light 22
Nature's Servant 23
Loosefall 24
Shopping 25
Jealousy 26
I Can See You 27

Nine-Liners

The Copper Beeches	31
Dead Trees	32
May	33
Fighting	34
Autopsy	35
Bar Scene	36
Gendered Discourse	37
Physics	38
Crossing the Street	39
Engrossed	40
Hillside	41
Life Stilled	42
Morning Mists	43
You on a Plane	44
Me on the Ground #1	45
Me on the Ground #2	46
The Social Me	47

Humiliations

Fear	51
On Feeling Despised	52
Calyx	53
Stiff Upper Lip?	54
Frustration	55
Arrivals	56
Communications	57
Fifteen Lines	58

Four-Liners

Headstrong	61
Succumbing	62
Summer's Heat	63
A Holiday Hope	64

Downcast 65
Stop-Loss 66
Bitterness.. 67
No-Man's Land 68

Let's Talk about the Weather

Slush Time 71
Ice Storm #1 72
Ice Storm #2 73
5:00 a.m. The Weather Forecast. Middle of March 74
End of March 2014 75
The Dusk of this Long Winter 76
Optimism... 77
Pumpkin Time 78

Old Age

I Have … 81
Youth and Old Age 82
Going into a Home 83
Does Wisdom Have an Age? 84

The Great Inequality

Discussion Group 87
"Say Not the Struggle Naught Availeth" 88
The Object of This Rhyme... 89
Fulcrum 90

Delilah

Impasse 93
I Live a Problem 94
The Night 95
I Failed 96
Nowhere to Go 97

Poems about Poetry

Forget It! 101
Drown Me Deep 102
Amuse-Gueule 103
A Vision of Fair Music 104
To All My Muses 105
Homage to Carlyle: The Battle of Quebec 106

About the Author 109

INTRODUCTION

This book is intended to be exactly what its title indicates—it is meant to be an extended apology to the heroine who inspired me to write to, for and about her in the Pursuit section of *Pursuit and Other Poems*, the Treading Water section of *Black Hole and Other Poems*, the My Inspiration section of *A Bell Curve and Other Poems*, and the whole of *An Artist's Model and Other Poems*. I made it clear in each of those volumes that my feelings for her were not reciprocated. But I have also realized what a nuisance my poetic advances must have been to her. So the current book is a bleak one, containing expressions of apology and remorse, but at the same time still expressing various kinds of desperate hope that *something* might come out of my efforts.

This book, therefore, presents a rather awkward attempt to come out from my impasse with at least some shreds of dignity. And of course what *was* left of my efforts were the poems listed above and the poems in this book.

The title of the very last poem in this book is "Homage to Carlyle: The Battle of Québec." In my previous book, *A Bell Curve and Other Poems*, there were a fair number of poems paying homage to poets of the past, but Thomas Carlyle (1795–1881) was predominantly a writer of prose. His masterpiece was titled *History of Friedrich II of Prussia, Called Frederick the Great*, and in it Carlyle had occasion to describe the Battle of Québec. In Canada in 1759, British troops under the leadership of General James Wolfe defeated French troops under the leadership of the Marquis Louis Montcalm. Readers may naturally wonder what a poem about a battle is doing in a collection of poems about romantic degradation, but its relevance to the rest of the book is made clear in its final stanza.

Another aspect of my attempt to escape my dilemma with some dignity was the development of something like a fascination with the actual *forms* the poems took. In the introduction to *Persistence and Other*

Poems, I described how I had discovered that four-line poems seemed to come into my mind spontaneously, so here I have gathered all the four-line poems (that emerged over the course of several months) into one section. Another section includes seventeen poems with a structure I have never used before, namely nine lines divided into three stanzas whose rhyme scheme is abc/ded/fff. And yet another section includes four "sprawl-verses," a form of blank verse that uses very short individual lines, most of which do not rhyme with any other lines. I derived this form, in particular, from my reading of lyrical poems by Heinrich Heine (1797–1856).

The very first poem, titled "Preamble: All I Can Do," sets the factual background for the rest of the book. The first seven sections, each of which contains a few poems, are called Apologies, Sprawl-Verses, Dangers, Nine-Liners, Humiliations, Four-Liners and Let's Talk about the Weather. Clearly, I am trying to crawl my way out of the depressed ambience of the first section, Apologies.

The last four sections are called Old Age, The Great Inequality, Delilah and Poems about Poetry. These represent my more abstract thoughts on these matters.

Once again, I must thank Marissa E. Barnes, a PhD candidate, and Rachel G. Murray, a professional librarian, for their assistance and support. I owe a particular debt of gratitude to Arnie Fernandez of iUniverse for providing extra help with the preparation of the manuscript for publication.

Preamble: All I Can Do

Oh for the years of yesteryouth,
When cares of undue age were nil
And the mere smile of a coquette,
Reciprocated, promised full
Fulfillment in a future yet
To be burdened by uncertainties!

But now, although my hair has thinned,
My cognitive press of rapture at
Passing glances and synchronies,
Depth-looks into eye hues that
Offer such sweet symmetries,
Yields only a moment's worth of Paradise.

All startings now lack structured future spine;
Fifty I look, but thirty is what I feel,
But nearer eighty I am in life and limb;
To no one, even you, dare I appeal
To be with me; all I can do is hymn
Your youth and brain and, dammit, yes, your eyes.

Apologies

An Apology

For all the stress I've brought to you,
I'm sorry; in a painting,
My head would be bent in a sorrow approaching abysmal.

For all the irritations I've caused you,
I'm sorry; in a mirror,
My eyes might glisten with tears of fear and remorse.

For being an onerous burden upon you,
I'm sorry; in a drama,
I'd movingly exit, the back of my hand on my brow.

For not being an uncle-like mentor and helper,
I'm sorry; in a movie,
I'd blush under arc lights for totally failing to be one.

For making you think I might be a jerk,
I'm sorry; in a video,
I'd brush from my shoulder the dandruff and dust of sheer rumour.

For loading you with my obsession with "Art!,"
I'm sorry; in a novel,
I'd be a nonhero for not being immodest enough.

But now, at last, I've caved in and ply you
With humble apologies here;
And I try to ignore the sensation the floor's not beneath me.

APOLOGY #2

This is a book of apprehended fears,
Fantasies caught in automatic light
And smothered in a mélange of regrets.

Cheer is missing; only now and then
A light-beam cluster-multiplex of flowers
Clarifies obscurity, then goes.

Ambition is faltering; for every stretch
Of high imagination and achievement,
A road of fallow dust lies underneath.

Hope glitters with the glances of my heroine
Or cannonades into a fen of doubt
Circled by rocks, each one a hollow timepiece.

No cheer is here, unless you read these words
As if they'd been carved on a wall of towering stone,
A monument relaying my mistakes;

And so I apologize for love unwise
And try to greet you, soliloquist that you are,
With generosity and consolation.

APOLOGY #3

Spread-eagled, I see my soul
Outlined against a sea-like sky
With a mighty stealth indicative
Of distrust of perfidiousness
And faith in the growth of groundswell heard below.

Honour I claim, not calumny,
For my actions, which were atavistic,
Forged from a Puritanical guilt;
Honour I claim for words that here express
An unrelenting wish to worship women,

But also in which my optimism falters
When *femmes fatales* are allotted the finest altars.

APOLOGY #4

I dare to hope that you'll accept
Apologies that I had kept,
Once my ego had seen through
The fact that I was bothering you.

Someone angry once said to me
How sad she knew that I would be
If I looked in a mirror, then had the thought
How stupid I'd been to ever have sought

The love of a lady half my age;
All my concoctions were persiflage
For a high-flown battle not to lose ground
In my fight to have a partner around.

My growing grey, my thinning hair,
My panting at the top of a stair,
My failing grip, my fears of the cold
That multiply as I grow old,

All testify, with a frightening truth,
That I'll never recoup the pride of my youth,
But, bumbling, go on my wearisome way
To where, in Elysium, water nymphs play.

REMORSE

A pallid tone pervades the every nook
And cranny of this unpretentious book.
I weep the thoughts of "what there might have been,"
Then wipe them out as if they were obscene.
Vainly I try, so hard I want to cry,
To compensate for what has flown me by.

Christmases sweeping earthlings off their feet,
Family outings where old strangers meet,
Premeditated trips with hope the goal,
Biographies to read that whet my soul,
And crossword puzzles ease my endless grind
Of trying to figure out what hit my mind.

Sprawl-Verses

GLITTER AND GLOSS

Who can deny
That glitter and gloss
And candy floss
Are wondrous to
A child's bright eye?

And who daren't assert
That refuse and dross
Are extra loss
To a man's dull eye
Who's losing his shirt?

'Tis 'twixt the two
That I ride aloft
On a surging swing,
Trying not to be soft.

Relativity Theory

Two kinds of time exist.
One is when
It's so far off before
I'll see you again
That counting the minutes or the days
Is a waste of time.
The other is when
It is so soon that I
Will see you again
That every minute of every day
Is saturated
Relentlessly
With joy that you'll return.

MEETING

Yesterday, when you arrived,
You smiled at me;
Not a fake smile,
But a real smile,
A smile vertiginous
In its arousal of
A smile by me
That mirrored yours
Reciprocally,
Unequivocally,
Unforced, unvirtual,
Resplendently real,
Yesterday, yesterday.

To the Sun

The winter sun,
Slowly sinking,
Plays a cold light
On patches of ice;
Frozen they stay.

But the same sun,
Beaming through my window,
Beatifies with warmth
The comfort-death
Of my two sofas.

O winter sun,
Elaborate, I pray
My poser-sitter's warmth
By shining on her through
A window warm with Utmost.

Dangers

Eye Contact

A blast-in forced by her piercing gaze
Took him by surprise,
Suggesting to her that he knew not the ways

Whereby a future promised touch
Might be for him if he
Were not to like her quite so very much.

And yet, the next time they met, he took,
Unplanned, a mock revenge;
A blast-in foisted on her by *his* look.

My Blast of Colour and Delight

My blast of colour and delight,
You fill with your infinite taste
And eternal eloquence each night
You are not here.

And I, in a gesture reprobate,
Dream of holding your waist
And savouring the aggregate
That makes it dear.

And the night swings pivotally;
The moon is quite outpaced;
Both blast my misplaced energy
And sneer.

The Psychopathology of Everyday Life

A "misadventure of sober gold"
Might be the name I could allot
To the time you phoned your parents but
Misdialed, and so their home was not
The place where your voice's magic spread;
It spread into my home instead.

And O, my sweetest bungle-child,
You laughed without apology
On reaching a thrilled but baffled me,
Who instantly thought, "Psychology!
A Freudian slip!" although I knew
That it had nothing at all to do

With a secret wish of yours to fill my ear
With the laughter and lilt you know I love to hear.

Female Eyes

Whenever you leave, I cannot think
Of anything except that I want
To keep you back and bundle you
Effusively, but no, I can't.

Your footfalls in the corridor
Are silently carpeted away,
Just as my dreams are when you go,
And I must wait for a later day,

When you'll return and look at me
With female eyes that peer and probe
Into my skull to see if I
Have feet still fettered to this globe

Or off to mental space off-ridden have,
Keeping my feelings hidden up my sleeve.

MY MODEL

I cannot *speak* of my astonishment
(For prose is a medium far too fused and flat),
When I see you seated, with your arms a-bare,
Wearing a T-shirt entrancingly too short,
Just where your arms and shoulders meet.

A blue of deeper blue than are most blues
Lies in its inherent mould to you; a power,
Though woefully weak in how it clings to you,
Is strong enough to break a lover's heart
Into a rain of fragments flung apart.

It symbolizes electricity
In how, when I see you, seated with arms a-bare,
I want to liaise your arms with artistry,
Beauty unending sitting facing me.

First Light

Once upon a solstice morning,
A placid sky lay over the lake, almost aching,
As if it felt the summer had blown by.

I thought it held a stagnant warning
That told me that my heart was almost breaking,
Until that "warning" showed itself a lie.

For I had felt a body-press adorning
Your greetings-hug, as if you thought of making
A freshened start toward a summer's sky.

NATURE'S SERVANT

A moment's growth, from hints to ecstasies,
Spotlights a sunburst in the eastern skies
That dazzles my sad and new-lacklustre eyes.

Hours later, a flawless eggshell blue
Colours the sky-lit canopy right through,
Resembling the ways my wishful thinkings do.

And last, when evening's darkness starshot is,
My mind rekindles hidden memories
Of cruelties among life's reveries.

LOOSEFALL

I cannot hold you to anything other
Than your project, self-proclaimed, to be
Free from the pressures of another,
Especially an oldster, such as me,

Who worships the carpets that you stand or walk on,
Who ogles the loosefall beauty of your hair,
Who thrills at every syllable your voice makes
As it sends its sounds to where I stand and stare.

Shopping

The wind that moves the meadows moves the land;
Oh, how I wish you'd consecrate your hand
To more than typing or tidying your hair
Or steering your car; please motivate your hand
To do for me what god-romantics planned.

And in appreciation, I'd reward
You with rings of lustrous silver drilled and bored,
Place necklaces round your neck with solemn care,
Accost uncommon vendors for their hoard
Of amulets with syllabaries scored,

And turn each move you make with any finger
Into a jewel on which your pride may linger.

Jealousy

If I too dim and unnoteworthy am
For you to squander your prudent mind's finesse
On me, then I apologize; and yes,
I dare expect no *soupcon* of caress.

But what if another sees my inner spark
And moves towards me, to hug, to hold, to squeeze,
While I reciprocate and heartily seize
Her armoured shoulders as strongly as I please?

Then may great Jealousy's pinions reach out,
And breach the atmosphere of your coldchest breath,
And fester your soul with a sort of daytime death,
Wherein I am unmentionable, shibboleth.

I Can See You

I fear that if I burden these poor walls
With more of my quasi-pubescent regrets,
They will call "Off!" and ask me to suppress
All of the sighs that desire for you begets.

For I can see you and know that only I
Can give you certain things that youth cannot;
And this is why I think you sometimes feel
Oppressed—because you have no antidote

That would smooth your mind and help to equalize
What tensions send more force from me to you
Than you to me; but then I feel your force
When you're in my sight; I enviously view

The curves of your head and your arms as you text
To somebody, somewhere, whatever it is you'll do next.

Nine-Liners

The Copper Beeches

The copper beeches on the hillside spark
With reddened dark the trees that still hold green
And the yellower willows dropping down to lawns.

The beeches are blasts of embryonic ore,
Waiting to be assembled into images
Of red things, blood and rosy-reds and gore.

Chattels of pain are not what the gods intended,
Unless, of course, they never had pretended
Other to be than mortal men upended.

Dead Trees

Dead trees betray a sort of mingled brown
When steadfastly displayed against a drape
Of living trees betrothed to swards of green.

My memory has antidotes to glee;
Brown visions of unhappy mental pain
Destroy what "reminiscence" means to me.

And so perhaps it also is for you;
A hoped-for cheer has melted into dew;
Your old mistrust of men has fired anew.

May

On the first sunny morning of this May,
The sky-bowl was an upturned potter's plate
Shot through with yellow where it wasn't blue.

On the first sunny morning of this May,
The sky-bowl seemed a resolute assertion
That, though we might quarrel, you would not go away.

On the first sunny morning of this May,
The sky-bowl shouted that you'd *want* to stay,
If only work could generate new play.

Fighting

Such visual beauty within a breath away!
Such emptiness all too visible within!
How absent you can seem when even here!

The landscape laughs out loud like a taunting youth;
Trees re-brandish branches that burst out
With powerhouse leaves and the ever-present truth

That spring cannot be stopped, only delayed.
My hopes resist being battled; they are made
Frailer, but somewhat stronger, when they're disarrayed.

AUTOPSY

Analysis, like a breathing breath of frost,
Casts its pure cloak of abandonment across
The achings of what-might-have-been-but-wasn't.

But all excuses, wild tergiversations,
Thinkings of why my intelligence choked my guts,
Excruciating rationalizations

Founder when brought up short against a wall
That asserts my pride was due a mighty fall;
Immoderation I lacked the most of all.

Bar Scene

Sobriety is such a mixed blessing
That I watch my friends succumbing to intemperance
And feel no sense of pride or win at all.

I went into a bar frequented by
Young people, but standing out from them
Were older men whom I could see would try

To pull and attract a woman-person who'd
Woo them away from their mournful singlehood
Into a world where both of them felt good.

Gendered Discourse

Schoolboys talking in their sundry ways
Amble between classes onto the wooded paths
That thread like ankle-length arteries through the park.

Were they talking ideas? Or books? Or smartphone trends?
Or how the spring is blossoming? Or sports?
Or parents? Or movies? Or college? Or friends?

All I saw as they walked was that they talked;
Their conversation was the kind at which I balked.
The girl who talked to herself was the kind I stalked.

Physics

The furthest shores of the lake have fineried themselves
With brown-mist swathes of linger-lying lastingness
Until, when the sun high-strikes, they fade and disappear.

Mere physics, devoid of feelings, pain or misty rue,
Determines those events, while I notate them here,
Ready to heap their symbols on my thoughts of you.

And you are off somewhere in the vastness of your space,
Determined to keep me here in this sequestered place,
Platonic, where I seethe with ill-disguised ill grace.

Crossing the Street

When I cross the street, I always look both ways
For oncoming vans swerving at me 'round corners
Or battle-geared cyclists swishing at me side-wise.

As I cross the street, I sometimes see fair women.
(One wore a dress of ravishing blue silk,
Making her more of a goddess than a human.)

But I am not encouraged if I try
To stop them to talk as they go rushing by.
If they want to talk, they'll give *me* the eye.

Engrossed

Boredom can never sap the roundelay
Of verses driven out of me when I think
Of you in your endless beauty watching me.

You know how totally engrossed I am
With thinking of what *could* be, if only
You could believe that every word I cram

Into my lines was serious, not a game.
If I drive you away by harping on the same
Irrationalities, then I'm to blame.

Hillside

There's nothing platitudinous about the way
Some tens of conifers and dozens of non-evergreens
Climb to small heights on the sloping hill to hide

Trellises and roofs and square-capped symmetries
From visibility; it artfully combines
Treetops and rooftops into a gullible synthesis.

And once, as I stood looking out, distracted, at that view,
I thought how to liken that house-dappled hillside to you:
You were both fashioned by Nature *and* Mind as you grew.

Life Stilled

I planted petunias, white and Tyrian purple;
I watered them first on an evening in May
When the sky was polished red with sunset clouds.

The morning next, with the lake a deadpan sheet
Of dawn-lit light, I went to water them
Again but felt my heart skip an unexpected beat

Because, face-down and dead, was an outspread bee.
Its abdomen shone black like ebony,
But its chest had been carrioned to a cavity.

Morning Mists

Five-thirty, and the sun cannot be seen;
Hidden behind engulfing clouds, it waits
And meanwhile churns aperitifs of grey,

Blotting with mists the balconies and blocks
Of buildings perched on the lake-cliffs' edge
That contrast with the tumblings of the rocks.

A thorny fog bedecks my windowpanes,
Forecast of hunger, forecast of new rains,
And augury of love destroyed by brains.

You on a Plane

Onto the landscape crawling by below
You fix your eyes, but landscapes don't stare back,
So anything erotic isn't there.

You press your hand to make your seat-back higher,
Shuffle your legs to give yourself more room,
And fiddle with your earphone and its wire,

While the low drone of the plane hums through
The seat, the window, even the lissom you,
Trying to remember what you'd forgotten to do.

ME ON THE GROUND #1

A massive mess of sunny thundercloud,
A brilliant white on top, a dark beneath,
Stretches across the skyline's afternoon.

The wind is strong, the petunias weave like mad,
Battered in their bins by blustery breezes,
As big a wind as they have ever had.

And, blown about like a flower in an urn,
By fears that never cease to chop and churn,
I count the lonely hours till you return.

Me on the Ground #2

Incorrigible wastes of high-flown verse
Are not incumbent harbingers of loss
But, rather, forecast a dearth of lively news.

Now you're away; I know I'll miss your speech,
With its golden monosyllables and flights
Of words on what you've learned on what you teach.

And maybe, perhaps, you'll miss me just a bit,
As in between the meeting rooms you flit,
Disdaining all temptations just to sit.

The Social Me

I'll never inveigle my way into your heart
Because, to get there, I'll have to troll your mind,
In order to prove you'll let me see your soul.

All I can do is be a social me,
Putting on normality like a flag
Of convenience that guarantees I'm free

To pester you with affection and sprinkle roses,
Confetti-like, over your artist's poses,
Swathing your life with beauty till it closes.

Humiliations

Fear

Long have my wanton verbal lootings climbed
To poem-cluttered peaks, where every touch
Or quiet, imagined look has raised a flag.
But now I fear a faltering of the drive,
A tendency for libido to leach away,
An ageing fall toward a smelly death,
An ending to intemperance and breath.

And so I want to wrestle-wrest a day
From this impending night and place its flame
Upright upon this topsy-turvy now
And let its blatant beams illuminate
A sadder, older me who wants to rage
Against the unwanted wastage of old age.

On Feeling Despised

So many nights I lie there and silently ask
How much disdain my colleagues feel for me,
That it's become a daily nocturnal task
To ask why failure should have dropped on me.

Was I too tough in demanding or not tough enough?
Was I too clever, or was I just obtuse?
Should I have excluded all mention of others to her?
Should I have refrained from excuse after feeble excuse?

Should I have held back and reduced my expressions of ardour?
Should I have shut up and, judiciously, silences kept
About my desire to hold her forever and ever
Through daytimes and nighttimes through which we deliciously slept?

I know that my life is weary and unkempt;
Even for myself I feel contempt.

Calyx

A calyx-cup to shape your voice
Is what my phone appears to be
When you call me.

A penetrating ache of hope
Fetters my voice's anarchy
When I reply.

And a lazy world goes back to sleep
When I reluctantly agree
To set you free.

Stiff Upper Lip?

Weeks of grey and dun and tan and drear
Had left a sky of cloud, a land unclear,
But a sudden sun has now unveiled the view
And left a vibrant sky so bright and new
That blacks and whites, not greys, predominate.

This promissory note is now my shout;
Things are re-brightening, shadows being shoved out.
I am recovering, hovering over a lake
Whose winds and mental waves converge to make
Propaganda for a newfound state

Wherein a status quo I must maintain,
Despite the fulminations of my brain.
On no account must I reveal designs
To flood you with a million Valentines.

Frustration

I have not even mock sublimity
To mould the gilded corners of my grief
That you are here, there, everywhere I look,
Yet not an inch of you you'll let me touch;
I think you push me from you overmuch.

So meanwhile on I go, a-looking outward,
Through mighty panes of glass at open air
And all things natural, obtrusive now
Because they symbolize what's inaccessible.
Outside vituperations irrepressible.

And so, like a lamb, pretending to be Blake-like,
I'll write of ineffabilities high and low
That greet my weary footsteps as I pad
With the onward steps recalcitrant and slow
Of a would-be lion who has nowhere to go.

Arrivals

Every day, as the day grows drear,
And the dusk grows arms to greet the night,
I know a day is drawing near
When I'll see you next, and such delight
Makes my heart rock with such anticipation
That my quiet hopes erupt into elation.

The elevator sounds grow more
As it rises to where you know I'll be;
At first, the light of its opening door
And a hint of your shadow is all I see.
And then you step, heart-throbbingly, into my sight,
And I know I'll not sleep for yet another night,

While I think how long it has been, and how often,
That I've seen you arrive and then leave but not soften.

Communications

No semaphore, a minimal signal,
Betrays its invincibility
In the way a sigh that surfaces out
Betrays a vulnerability.

No Internet, no megabyte,
Betrays its bits of shallowness
In the way a yawn that bursts its bank
Betrays erotic fallowness.

No jangled ring of telephone
Betrays its interruptive power
In the way a gruntlike silent snore
Betrays a longed-for treasured hour.

Sounds are like silences magnetized
To underscore with pain those times
You'd hoped to value, but instead
Found empty of rhythm and barren of rhymes.

Fifteen Lines

"Tomorrow" or "tomorrow" or "tomorrow"
Are all "todays" wherein I hide a tear,
But like a dove a-bubbling good cheer,
I'll set myself to greet you warmly here,
Because, though sad I've been for over a year,
I'm now a-bustling, trying to ease your fear,
Given you used to dread the atmosphere
When I displayed desire if you stood near.
But now I'm older, calmer, more sincere.
I hesitate before I call you "dear,"
Knowing you might demur, and so I steer
Our talk onto your work and your career.
But all this cogitation is a mere
Addendum to the hours when I appear
A hostage to today until tomorrow.

Four-Liners

HEADSTRONG

Once I knew someone whose earnest intellect
Completely failed to charm or to attract
The little blonde he'd set his heart upon.
How do I know? *She* told me why she'd gone.

SUCCUMBING

I find fantastic science in your gaze,
Sweet arts of every vulnerable kind
In your lips, and a gossamer gate
So tightly closed I nearly lose my mind.

Summer's Heat

When summer's heat is herald of the heart
And sunlight bears down upon the busy street,
Even a poet exuding newborn verses
Must try to be dispassionate, discreet.

A Holiday Hope

A holiday hope that will not die
Encourages all earth and sky
To put aside all childish dreams
In reverence when the sun strides by.

Downcast

A marigold lies weeping
Under a lavender sky,
While fertility lies sleeping,
Wondering why.

Stop-Loss

Tidal friction, loose and rippled,
Demarcates the end of start;
Tidal friction, tight and fissured,
Designates a broken heart.

Bitterness

A lazy interface of light
Extends each dawned and dreadful day
Into the concourse of a night
Where psychic pain won't go away.

No-Man's Land

There are winds that bluster through
The veils of no-man's land;
When love makes war on hate,
Anger, not greed, is in command.

Let's Talk about the Weather

Slush Time

How deeply dark and subtly mystical
Was the aftermath, for me, of your sudden call.
After you'd fallen onto a furrowed slush
From a spill on a whisper of a wisp of ice,
And found yourself bedraggled, unbecoming,
Wet, and maybe bruised, you rose and stepped
To where you could ease yourself (or tumble) into
The seat of your still-warm car, and, shaken sick,
Phoned me, with voice determined, to assert
You needed to go back home. I "yessed" unquestioning,
Knowing, from my own confusion after falling,
How strength and a sturdy urge to enterprise
Would only return after a rest in the true
And brooding bosom of all care, one's home.

Ice Storm #1

Thousands of bristles of spindly candles
Render candescent the slope of the hill;
The sun on the lake is brilliant-flat,
And the sun on the trees strikes steady and still,
Turning each bristle, each thistle of ice
To a brushstroke inferno of white Paradise.

The ardent assembly of crystalline thousands
Will scintillate silvers till prickly Night
Drops, in untalented darknesses bold,
Upon each of the slivers of candlelike light,
A shininess ready to catch the glows
Of Christmassy reds and greens on the snows

Till daylight, dull daylight, capped in dark grey,
Bleaches the ice show and drains it away.

Ice Storm #2

Must I then, now, myself for death prepare?
In an ice-storm blackout, halfway down the stair
From the fourteenth floor, my flashlight fizzled out,
And in pitch-blackness, there I sat, pooped out,

Too tired to lug my bag for overnights,
Its books and clothes and shoes down six more flights.
Puffed with fatigue, I sat, yes, feeling shame,
Till, armed with flashlights, two young people came

To escort me downstairs to the lit ground-level floor,
And out along that ground floor's corridor
To where my family waited with their car,
To drive me to a room I'd booked before

I'd decided to dare that dreadful down-stair trip
Where my burned-out flashlight was just another slip
On this junkyard road at the closing of my life
Whose jostlings unamorous can't match a living wife.

5:00 A.M. THE WEATHER FORECAST. MIDDLE OF MARCH

No rain today and a bright-white moon
Tempt me to write "She'll be driving here soon,"
But a brisk white ribbon on the TV road
From there to here shows the driving's slowed
And the numbers at the bottom of the TV screen
Are indicators of the snow that's been.

And day after day it's been like this,
Numbers and measures of shop-talk bliss
Smashed against others of snow, rain, and hail,
Asserting that Nature doth choose to exhale
Her benighted breath on this whited land,
Determined to smash all my dreams into sand.

But riveting, like Justice or Hope or Despair,
My dreams to the real is the fact you're still there.

End of March 2014

Oh, how slowly this onset summer's taking
To make up its mind to be here
And sing out, loud and clear,
That summer sunsets mock us in their making!

Night has a fervour now to cloud the moon;
Its mistinesses rush
Tamely to tar and brush
Tall-standing stars with essences of June.

And Night will stagger on into July,
To when the cloudless sky
Will balefully stand by
To load the world with a winter cold and dry,

While lines like these decay away and fade,
Unless a Muse protests
That nothing else attests
To truth so well as does a serenade.

The Dusk of this Long Winter

"The Little Bigness that Couldn't"
Is the name of a poem I know I shouldn't
Write, for fear I'm portrayed forever
As a powerless poet who's unpleasantly clever.

So let the dusk of this long winter's shroud
Descend in a cloak of fathomless cloud
To cover the somnolent earth with appraisals
Of schemings gone wrong and "Why me?" reprisals.

And all of the murk that Intellect pours
Onto seekers who seek to find open doors
To renewals or onto intriguers and wooers,
Who scream to get rid of the dusk of those boors,

Who find that every move they think is ruthless,
Is merely poignant, brash, or empty, toothless.

Optimism

I wandered where the stars seemed close to home
On summer nights, unless the cloud lines blocked
The darker sky behind them and thus locked
The stars into a self-built pleasure-dome—

Such optimism, given that the stars
Had always been, for me, the silent tears
Wept from the womb of heaven when arrears
And jiltings made my hopes mere avatars—

Such optimism, given that the skies
Of Canada in no wise replicate
Those that, in Europe, try to eradicate
The cruelties that colour Europe's histories—

My optimism rose because I saw you smile,
As if you'd logged on to my mid-Victorian style.

Pumpkin Time

A slate-grey blue and ochre-tinted green
Stand out as unexpected novelties
In the spread
Of autumn's standard colours, gold and red,
So prolix in the fall's frivolities;

At the moment when you unexpectedly said
You would have felt like I did in my choice
Of a lumpy
Pumpkin to be carved all weird and grumpy,
My world perked up at the silver of your voice.

And I was silent, rapt for one pure second;
A thought-beam flashed across my busy mind,
Candescent,
Like a revelation iridescent,
That we, more than you knew, might be of a kind.

Old Age

I Have …

I have a deep, unfathomable drive
Whose plummeted deeps will never be addressed
Except in words tangential at their best.

That drive had started in childhood's depths
And risen, through biographies unexpressed,
Up to its old-man's state of over-zest.

Youth and Old Age

The tragic force of overgrown old age
Destroying, with ineffable compliance,
The very roots of mutual *homage*
And all decorum in erotic matters,
Stretches its tentacles to mutilate
Even our mutual interests in the sciences,
In history, and even in the arts.

For, when I walk, I walk at greater ease
With someone older than you, less pliable.
I stand, turgid, with a half-full glass,
While party-melting chatter buzzes 'round.
But you propel yourself, with happy banter,
From person to person, *liking* socializing,
While Youth to you its treasury imparts.

Going into a Home

Sidling into a maudlin death is not
What my creator-mind had planned for me;
A triumph-death, a martyr-death, a century-
Death looks better in a eulogy.

But to bumble about, needing help to eat,
Assistance to put on my old-man's clothes,
A stick to help me stalk my way up steps,
All of these would be appalling blows

That would lock me in unwelcomed space and time.
Ideals would be symbolized by books unread,
And dramas by the weather news, and food
By puréed everything I'd be fed.

And my bed would have two sheets with not a hint
That a woman of mine had left her body-print.

Does Wisdom Have an Age?

Let no worthy rumours brook
Atrocities that rose and took
Extremities of happenstance
As models for a worthy book.

Never was putrefying blood
A healthy wind blowing somebody good;
Only the solace of embrace
Brings mind to body's humanhood.

Let no worthy rumours brook
Atrocities that rose and took
Extremities of happenstance
As models for a worthy book.

The Great Inequality

Discussion Group

I do not have the wherewithal to fend
For myself in a world where conflicts always tend
To arise when, seated at a table made for ten,
Old rivalries are re-unleashed again.

And if my voice seems, well, unconfident,
At least your silence is quite kindly meant;
But if I say one word on inequality,
Murderous looks enmesh my hapless me.

"Say Not the Struggle Naught Availeth"

When Westerners fight beneath an Eastern sun,
They're fighting men who, since their tribes began,
Have scrabbled to keep and hold dominion
Over the women of Afghanistan.

And every time an ankle smooth appears
Just for a moment beneath a massive skirt,
Desire wins out over forgettable fears,
And Death sets new stepping-stones into the dirt.

The Object of This Rhyme

The Great Inequality is what I make
The object of this rhyme; make no mistake,
The mysteries of virtuosity
Are nothing next to never feeling free.

For liberty could never be a sin
Deeper than the wrong that Truth is in
When Inequality is made a right
So wrong that even angels flee its sight.

Fulcrum

I have retained no fulcrum of balance;
The world is jovially set to dance
And greet new freedoms with a joyous spree,
But I feel forced to remain my joyless me.

And yet, perhaps, enchantment still might come
Where I can hide, unrebuffed, while some
Of the joys of yesteryouth return,
And I feel the welter-worlds of love reburn,

While my partner, I hope, feels something too;
Under my pillow I'll thrust "Indifference" through
With a mental melancholic sword part rusty,
But only part; I can still call it "trusty"

And, in a blissful anonymity,
Continue my fight with Inequality.

Delilah

Impasse

There is a high, peculiar branch
Of whoredom where her men don't fight
But share her affections at her will.

There's also a miserable class
Of whorelike poets who glamorize
All women at whom they make a pass.

And, lastly, there's a worldly kind
Of female, widely read, refined,
Who cannot stand a poet's mind.

I Live a Problem

I live a problem of weakness thwarted,
Of strength restrained, because I hate
The cloud of stark morality
Suffusing my putrid mind of late.

When, through the veils of a long-lost distant night,
I see thee creep, Delilah, to thy den,
I want to caress thy silken-smoothness hair,
But still I hate myself, yes, even then.

The Night

Twenty times a star has tolled destruction,
And moons have steered in sled-like masquerades
Over the wide and wearied clouds of night.

Dost thou, Delilah, worship them, as softly
Thou pressest a finger near the mouthing part
Of thine orifice, praying that the night

Will softly drain his effervescent opening
Into thy suffused and posed *entrada*,
That part of thee entranced by the night?

I Failed

Oh what a bloody gloom befalls
Those errant corners of my mind
Where you are locked in a memory clinch
With happiness I've failed to find!

All other corners are untouched
By malice, gossip or shaming joy;
But where you are, in your corner steeped,
You prove, Delilah, you employ

A thousand tricks you think that I
Can sympathize with, but all in vain.
I'm sick to death of finding girls
Who turn my moral scruples into pain.

Nowhere to Go

A house refilled with pleasurable art
Does little to assuage my riven heart,
Nor can bright knickknacks on a mantelpiece
Veil the venality of your masterpiece
Of treachery found in arms that were not mine
That held and infused you with lechery divine.

I have nowhere to go to quench my grief.
If I am kind, this gives me no relief;
If I am cruel, you've won and dragged me down
To where your vileness masquerades as clown;
If I run for help, I simply confirm your guess
That weakness underlies my tenderness.

And if I go on as if nothing had taken place,
I'm burdened for life with incipient disgrace.

Poems about Poetry

FORGET IT!

There is no better antidote
To poetry than taking note
And memorizing what you wrote
Within some verse or anecdote.

Remember them, though, and you will find
They occupy and fill your mind
So forcefully that any kind
Of newborn verse remains confined

To a state of nonexistingness,
A nothing filled with emptiness,
And, consequently, you'll know less
Of any poetry success

Because *your* stuff you've learned by heart
Snuffs out your newborns at their start.

Drown Me Deep

Oh, drown me deep in devastating dirt;
Ply me with novel come-ons as we flirt.
Remind me to remember to adjust my shirt,
And keep me rapt forever with your skirt;
For what's not reproductive is inert.

Amuse-Gueule

A haiku with exactly
Seventeen syllables
Isn't spontaneous.

A haiku with ex-
Actly seventeen syllab-
Les isn't spontaneous.

A haiku that ex-
Plodes with mysteriosity
Is spontaneous.

A Vision of Fair Music

A balcony seat above a concert hall
Gave me occasion to scan the crowd below.
A red dress and a golden heft of hair
Did not blend in with the emollient ambience
Of the others around but stood apart as if
To overture the music we would hear.

A testament to the history of light
Is what that hair may soon be made to bear;
And that dress of pressing red announces loud
That its wearer wants herself to see and feel
The manly beauty and the manly beast
That lurk alike in male and female songs.

And so I think the upshot of my vision
Will be more Beethoven and less derision.

To All My Muses

To start a quietly sceptr'd mount of gold,
A radiant jewel upon a mountainside,
Weathers must mingle the dusty with the trite,
And, overarching, the sky must spread its stride.

And thus it is, humbly, at the entrance
To a redacted, polished, burnished cave
That I set down this boding of a venture
To place you all on an odic architrave,

Features in a frieze around a temple,
An architecture spawned of living verse.
But flat-laid is the simulated building;
It does not dominate the pluriverse

Of little things poetic, burred and bold;
It stands, instead, sustained in missal'd starlight,
A gallantry torn from novelties grown old
And newnesses redestined to delight.

Homage to Carlyle: The Battle of Quebec

I stood beside Wolfe's monument in England
And saw the vivid past array its ranks
Across the house-thick serried rows of hedges
That stretched beyond the sun-shot Thames to where
The countryside of England lent its corners
To fenland acres and the Suffolk coast.

I also thought of where I'd stood, in Canada,
In a courtyard held up high above a river
Quadruple to the Thames in width and broadness,
With hills like mountains when the sky grew grey;
A river wherein swam whales and not just fish,
And where be-bonneted heroines and nuns
From Normandy had grown their sacred hedges
With a vehemence unique to pioneers.

A statue in that courtyard stood and gazed
Over the *seigneuries* of tilled Québec.
Like Wolfe's, this statue gazed across *his* landscape,
Where the sun set gingerly, between low clouds,
Spreading a light that petered out in winter,
While he, Louis Hébert, beheld his work,
His settlements, and pronounced them very good.

Wolfe's conquest of the Heights of Abraham,
In 1759 was an unintended
Consequence of a far-off state of warfare,
The Seven Years' War, in which Québec and Canada
Had really no prior need to take a part;
The war was Prussians versus Austrians,
But it spilled cantankerously to *La Nouvelle France*.

Wolfe battered Québec with siege guns for six weeks;
Montcalm, we know from a letter back to France,
Knew well he could lose if Wolfe took enterprise
And climbed the heights in stealth, the which Wolfe did.
And the Brits had bayonets, lacking to Québecers,
And thereby won the hand fights on the Heights.

But Montcalm was smiling, even as he died, because,
Within ten years, his letter said, resentful younger sons
And Englishmen impoverished back home,
Who had found a handle to a future stardom
In the rough woods and sunshine of America,
Would break their bond with a king and with a country
That seemed to care too little for their comfort;
Rebellion would strike down colonies' ramparts;
So Wolfe would not have the last laugh after all.

But it's also in Carlyle we find a Wolfe-craft,
A sentence that overstraddles thoughts of war,
For with him Wolfe had brought a slender volume,
A book full packed with Wisdom's take on death,
Gray's *Elegy*, now resting calm in a library,
But blazed by Wolfe as "Melody Eternal."
Wolfe hoped to thank heaven, were he to win Québec,
As much as any poet would who'd written Gray;
In dimming death, a poet held Wolfe's hands.

About the Author

David J. Murray has published nine books of poetry as well as scholarly books, articles and encyclopedia entries. Born and raised in Manchester, England, he earned a doctorate at the University of Cambridge. Dr. Murray is currently emeritus professor of psychology at Queen's University, Kingston, Ontario, and a resident of Toronto.

Printed in the United States
By Bookmasters